MW01123317

FIRE

Gabrielle Woolfitt

Wayland

Titles in this series
Air
Earth
Fire
Water

TOPIC CHART

	SCIENCE*	ENGLISH	MATHS*	TECHNOLOGY	GEOGRAPHY	HISTORY	PHYSICAL EDUCATION	MUSIC	ART	RELIGIOUS EDUCATION
What is fire?										
Cooking fires				AT L4–5	✔					
Volcanoes	AT 3 L5	AT 2 L4			AT 3 L5	AT 3 L2–5				
How hot?			AT 2 L4–5						✔	
Messages and symbols		AT 1 L2–3				CSU 5	✔			
Fires and farming					AT 4 L4 AT 5 L4–5					
Holy flames						✔				✔
Fire beasts	AT 2 L2	AT 3 L2–5								
Burning	AT 3 L2–5									
Fires that destroy					AT 2 L4	AT 1 L3–4				
The sun	AT 3 L1–5	AT 3 L2–5				CSU 1,5,6				
Painting fires									✔	
Building a 3 stone stove				AT 3 L2–3	✔					
Fire sounds		✔						✔		

KEY CSU = Core Study Unit AT = Attainment Target L = Level * Proposed ATs, October 1991

First published in 1992 by
Wayland (Publishers) Ltd
61 Western Road, Hove
East Sussex BN3 1JD, England

© Copyright 1992 Wayland (Publishers) Ltd

Editor: Cath Senker
Designer: Helen White
Consultant: Tom Collins
Deputy Headmaster of St Leonards
CEP School, East Sussex

British Library Cataloguing in Publication Data

Woolfitt, Gabrielle
Fire – (The elements)
I. Title II. Series
541.361

ISBN 0 7502 0354 4

Typeset by White Design
Cover and inside artwork by Maureen Jackson.
Printed by G. Canale & C.S.p.A. Turin
Bound in France by A.G.M.

CONTENTS

Words printed in **bold** are explained in the glossary.

WHAT IS FIRE?

ABOVE, **The space shuttle burns lots of fuel to help it lift off into space.**

When something burns it produces fire. Fires are always hot. Look at this space shuttle taking off. How hot do you think the tail fire is? Why do rockets need fire?

Fire is dangerous. Fire can spread quickly. Whole forests can burn down because a careless person drops a match. A house can burn down if an accident happens in the kitchen. You must always respect fire and treat it with care. Then you will be safe.

SYMBOLS AND MESSAGES

The Olympic flame is a special symbol of the Olympic Games. The Olympic flame always burns on Mount Olympus in Greece, where the games started over 2,000 years ago. Every four years the flame is carried from Mount Olympus to the stadium where the games are held. When the Olympic flame is burning the games can begin.

Fire is used for carrying other types of message. Native Americans used to send messages by smoke signals. They had an alphabet of signals, rather like **Morse code**.

Beacon fires used to be lit in Britain to spread important messages – about the death of a king or an invasion of the country.

Imagine a fire burning on top of a hill. Many people can see the fire. A person 30 km away makes a fire on another hill. More people can see this fire. In turn they light more beacon fires. In this way an important message could be passed around England in about half an hour.

OPPOSITE **This is the Olympic flame burning at the Olympic Games in Seoul in 1988.**

FIRES AND FARMING

Fires can be useful in farming. In the forests of South America many people grow some of their food in food plots. They make the food plots by cutting down trees in a small area and then burning the plants.

ABOVE **Maize is growing in this food plot in a forest in Brazil.**

Crops grow in the plots for a few years. Then new plots are made somewhere else and the forest grows back. This is called slash and burn farming. When a large area is cleared it can harm the forest.

Some industries are responsible for cutting down and burning huge areas of forest. They grow corn or raise cows for beef to sell in other countries. They keep using the land until there is no goodness left in the soil. The forest cannot grow back.

In many countries crops are grown in fields. When the harvest has been gathered, plant stems and roots are left. This is called stubble. In Britain farmers used to burn it. The ash that was left was good for the soil. But the government decided to stop burning stubble, because it made dirty smoke which polluted the air.

ABOVE **The orange flames spread quickly along the rows of stubble.**

HOLY FLAMES

BELOW **These candles light up an old oil painting of Mary and Jesus in a Russian Church.**

Fire is a symbol of light in Christianity. Light keeps away the dark and evil. Candles are burnt in some churches. The flames give a soft orange light.

As the smoke rises it helps to carry peoples' thoughts and prayers to heaven. **Incense** is burnt in Catholic churches. It makes a strong, sweet smell which helps to soothe and calm people while they pray.

Fire is also used by Hindus when a person dies. Rajiv Gandhi was killed in 1991. He had been the Prime Minister of India, and was a Hindu. His body was burnt on a **funeral pyre** but his spirit was released. The ashes were poured into the River Ganges. Hindus believe that his spirit will go into a new body as a baby. This is called reincarnation.

ABOVE **The body of Rajiv Gandhi was carried slowly through the crowds on its way to the funeral pyre.**

FIRE BEASTS

ABOVE **Dragon dancers still perform in some countries. This group is in Singapore.**

In stories there are many kinds of fire beasts, but there are no real animals which can live in fires.

In many countries there are **myths** about dragons. Most dragons are magical. Some can breathe fire. Chinese dragons are old and wise. The Chinese year of the dragon comes every twelve years. If you were born in 1976 or 1988 you are a dragon person. It is supposed to be lucky to be a dragon person.

There is a mythical creature called a salamander, that lives in every fire and keeps it alight. Salamanders are **guardians** of the flames. If you look long and hard at a log fire you may see the salamander in the glowing **embers**!

Another famous fire beast is the phoenix. The myth says that the phoenix can set fire to itself and be burnt to ashes, but will rise again after 500 years. Write a story about a salamander or a dragon – or invent your own fire beast.

BELOW **This is a statue of the Lord of Fire, worshipped by the Aztec people long ago in Mexico.**

BURNING

BELOW **The flame burns slightly above the surface of the fuel because the oxygen and the fuel cannot mix inside the match.**

How does something burn? Fuel, heat and oxygen are needed to make a fire. A fuel is anything that can burn, like wood or coal. Heat is a type of energy that makes things hot. Oxygen is a gas that is all around us in the air.

Watch a match burning. The wood is the fuel, the heat comes from the chemicals in the match head,

and oxygen comes from the air. If you blow on the match you cool it down. You take away the heat so the match goes out.

When all the wood has burnt there is no more fuel, so the match goes out. If you put a plate on top of the match the fire runs out of oxygen and goes out. Make a poster to show how things burn.

If you understand the fire triangle you can put fires out. You must take away either the fuel, the heat or the oxygen, and then the fire will die.

ABOVE **Some rocks contain metal. The metal is produced by heating the rocks in a very hot fire called a smelter. This smelter is in Botswana.**

FIRES THAT DESTROY

A small fire can spread quickly and go out of control. Fire can destroy houses, forests or even a whole town. The fire of London burnt most of the city. It started in a baker's shop early in the morning of 2 September 1666. The fire spread easily because most of the houses were built of wood and they were close together.

It took three days to put out the fire and many people died. In the end sailors knocked down wooden houses in the fire's path so they could not catch light.

More than 100,000 people lost their homes in the fire, but some good came out of it. The germs that had caused the **Plague** were destroyed. London was rebuilt with wider streets and houses of brick and stone.

BELOW **In this painting of the fire of London, people who have escaped the fire are watching it from the river bank near the Tower of London.**

There are still some kinds of fire which are very difficult to put out. During the Gulf War in 1991 Kuwaiti oil wells were set alight. These fires were so hot that the sand nearby melted.

Nobody could go close enough to put the fires out. Black smoke filled the sky and blocked out the sun, so it was often dark during the day.

Find out about some other big fires. What damage did they cause? How were they put out?

ABOVE **A fire fighter stands behind a screen while he works out how to put out the flames.**

THE SUN

Most of the world's energy comes from the sun. It is 150 million km (93 million miles) away from the earth. Light from the sun travels through space until it reaches the earth. The light is a form of energy. It heats our planet.

ABOVE **In Norway at the end of June, the sun does not set, it just dips towards the horizon. The further north you go, the better you can see the midnight sun.**

The sun is a star. A star is a huge ball of very hot gases. The gases react with each other and this makes light and heat. Some people say the sun is a ball of flames, but this is not true. There is no oxygen on the sun, so it cannot be burning.

Without the sun's energy nothing could live on earth. Many people have worshipped the sun – from the Ancient Egyptians to the Incas in Peru. The Ancient Greeks said that the sun was a burning chariot that rode across the sky every day.

The sun can tell us what time of day it is. Find out how a **sundial** works.

Remember, you should never look directly at the sun, as it can hurt your eyes.

BELOW **These people are making offerings to the Sun God during the Inti Raymi festival in Cuzco, Peru.**

PAINTING FIRES

This picture shows the burning of a palace. It was painted in Japan hundreds of years ago. What do you think of the way that the flames are shown?

Compare the various pictures of fires in this book. Sometimes the flames are sooty and orange.

Other fires have blue flames. The hottest fires have almost white flames. Watch the flame as a twig burns. Watch how a candle burns. Look at films or videos of fires.

Painting fire is very difficult. Fires are always moving. Even the fire on a gas cooker sways and hisses as it burns. Fires are always bright. You might need to use poster paint or thick pastels to create a strong picture – or use strips of tissue paper.

First, decide what kind of fire to paint. How big is it? What is burning? What colours can you see? Is there any smoke? Try to show the flames moving.

ACTIVITIES

Build a three-stone stove.
Ask an adult to help you with this outdoor project.
1. Find three large stones. They should be flat on the top and the bottom.
2. Put them in a triangle on a piece of concrete or on bare earth. Make sure you can balance a pot on the three stones.
3. Put dry twigs, dried grass and old newspapers into the space between the stones. This is the fuel.
4. You could try to light the fire by rubbing a stick into a groove on a piece of wood. Or you could use matches!
5. Once the fire has started, put on some larger pieces of wood.
6. Place a pot half-filled with water on the stones. See if you can keep the fire going for long enough to cook some spaghetti!

Fire Sounds

London Bridge is Burning Down is an English nursery rhyme about fire. Can you think of some more poems or songs about fire? You could make up some music that sounds like fire.

How could you make the sounds of something catching fire? Fire crackles. You could use paper or tree branches to make these sounds. Try playing some percussion instruments. Use your voice as well.

Sometimes ashes and coals drop away from the fire. If it is a big fire a whole building could collapse. When the fire has died only smoke remains.

Could you produce the sounds of a fireworks display? Think of the various kinds of fireworks and the noises they make.

Record your fire music. Ask other people to listen and see if they can tell what is happening.

GLOSSARY

Blast furnace A tower with a very hot fire which is used to melt metals.

Embers Small pieces of coal or wood left glowing after a fire.

Erupt To explode or burst out.

Freezing point The temperature at which a liquid turns into a solid.

Funeral pyre A platform made of wood, used for burning dead bodies in some countries.

Guardian A person who looks after something or someone.

Incense A substance which gives off a strong smell when burnt.

Mains Gas, water or electricity that is piped straight into buildings.

Morse code A system of signalling using sounds or flashes of light.

Myth An ancient story about gods and very strange events.

Plague A serious disease that killed thousands of people around the world in the seventeenth century.

Sundial A kind of clock that uses a shadow made by the sun to show what time it is.

FINDING OUT MORE

Books

Death Customs by Jon Mayled (Wayland, 1986)
The Fire of London by Rupert Matthews (Wayland, 1988)
Global Warming by Laurence Pringle (Hodder and Stoughton, 1990)
Greek Myths and Legends by C. Evans (Usborne, 1985)
Rainforests by Sue Hadden (Wayland, 1991)
Volcano by John Dudman (Wayland, 1992)
Volcano by B. Knapp, World Disasters Series (Macmillan, 1989)

Computer software

Dragon World by 4mation, Education Resources, Linden L.E.A.,
Rock Park, Barnstaple, Devon EX32 9AQ
Firewise (Fire prevention for children) by the Home Office, Room 133,
50 Queen Anne's Gate, London SW1H 9AT

Music

Firedance by Manuel de Falla (Essential Classics, Volume 1)

Teachers' resources

Sun, Moon and Stars, Science Mini Unit (Scholastic, 1991)
A Unit about Dragons (Scholastic)

INDEX

Page numbers in **bold** indicate subjects shown in pictures, but not mentioned in the text on those pages.

Picture Acknowledgements
The publishers would like to thank the following for allowing their illustrations to be used in this book: Allsport (P. Rondeau) 12; Bruce Coleman *cover*, (E. Pott) 5 (bottom), 24, (G. Moore) 20, (T. O'Keefe) 25; Geoscience Features 8; Hutchison 14, 16 (bottom), 21; Photri 4; Popperfoto 16 (top); Frank Spooner Pictures 23 (top); Tropix 6; Wayland Picture Library 11 (right), 22, (A. Blackburn) 10, 27, 28, 29, (T. Woodcock) 11 (left); Werner Forman Archive 19, 26; ZEFA (R. Bond) 7, 15, (Damm) 18.